DISCARDED

NOTE TO PARENTS

Welcome to Kingfisher Readers! This program is designed to help young readers build skills, confidence, and a love of reading as they explore their favorite topics.

These tips can help you get more from the experience of reading books together. But remember, the most important thing is to make reading fun!

Tips to Warm Up Before Reading

- Ask your child to share what they already know about the topic.
- Preview the pages, pictures, sub-heads, and captions, so your reader will have an idea what is coming.
- Share your questions. What are you both wondering about?

While Reading

- Stop and think at the end of each section. What was that about?
- Let the words make pictures in your minds. Share what you see.
- When you see a new word, talk it over. What does it mean?
- Do you have more questions? Wonder out loud!

After Reading

- Share the parts that were most interesting or surprising.
- Make connections to other books, similar topics, or experiences.
- Discuss what you'd like to know more about. Then find out!

With five distinct levels and a wealth of appealing topics, the Kingfisher Readers series provides children with an exciting way to learn to read about the world around them. Enjoy!

Ellie Costa, M.S. Ed.
Literacy Specialist, Bank Street School for Children, New York

KINGFISHER READERS

level
4

Rivers

Claire Llewellyn and Thea Feldman

KINGFISHER
NEW YORK

Series editor: Thea Feldman
Literacy consultant: Ellie Costa, Bank Street College, New York

ISBN: 978-0-7534-7124-1 (HB)
ISBN: 978-0-7534-7125-8 (PB)

Kingfisher books are available for special promotions and
premiums. For details contact: Special Markets Department,
Macmillan, 175 Fifth Ave., New York, NY 10010.

For more information, please visit
www.kingfisherbooks.com

Printed in China
9 8 7 6 5 4 3 2 1
1TR/1013/WKT/UG/105MA

Contents

What is a river?   4

The flowing river   6

The water cycle   8

Shaping the land   10

River plants   12

River animals   14

Rivers and people   16

Using river water   18

Rivers and floods   20

Dams and water power   22

River transportation   24

Enjoying the river   26

Taking care of rivers   28

Glossary   30

Index   32

What is a river?

Rivers are bodies of **fresh water** that flow to the sea. They can be very different from each other. Some rivers flow quickly, and others move slowly. Some rivers are narrow streams. Others are so wide that you cannot see from one side to the other. A river may be all of these things at different places along its route.

Rivers are great for kayaking and other water sports.

Rivers are homes for animals and plants. They are important to people, too. We travel on them. We build towns on their **banks**. We take fish from them for food, and we use river water for all sorts of things.

Kingfishers build their nests on riverbanks and feed on freshwater fish.

In this book you will find out about how rivers change as they flow to the sea and about how powerful they can be when they flood the land.

Record-breaking rivers

The Nile River (right) is the world's longest river. It is 4,160 miles (6,695 kilometers) long. The D River in Oregon is the shortest. It is just two-tenths of a mile (37 meters) long—the length of seven canoes.

The flowing river

The place where a river starts is called its **source**. From the source, a river flows downhill on its journey to the sea. The path the river takes is called its **course**.

The river's starting place, or source, is high up in the mountains.

The river moves fast as it flows downhill.

The river gets bigger as other rivers and streams join it.

The river's mouth

The place where a river empties into the sea is called the river's **mouth**. There is often a lot of mud there. Birds come to the mouth and push their beaks into the mud. They pull out snails, worms, and other juicy creatures.

An **estuary** is a part of the sea that cuts into the land to meet the mouth of a river.

The river reaches flatter ground and slows down. It becomes wider and deeper. It snakes in big curves called **meanders**.

The water cycle

The water on our planet is constantly being **recycled**. It is always moving between the sea, the air, and the land. This movement is called the **water cycle**, and rivers are an important part of it.

1. The water cycle starts with the Sun. Its heat changes water on the surface of the land and sea into a gas. The gas is called **water vapor**.

2. Water vapor rises up into the sky, where the air is colder.

Recycled water

The water cycle has recycled the same water for billions of years. So the water that you drink today may once have been a drink for a dinosaur, sipping at a river!

3. The vapor turns back into droplets of water and forms clouds.

4. Droplets in the cloud join together and fall as rain.

5. The rain runs into rivers, and the cycle starts again.

Shaping the land

Rivers follow the shape of the land, but they can also change it. Moving water is very powerful. As a river flows over the land, it picks up stones and even boulders. These roll along with the water. They carve the **riverbed** and chip away at the banks, making the river deeper and wider. This carving and chipping is called **erosion**.

This river in New Zealand flows so rapidly that it can move boulders.

Sometimes it is the land that changes a river. When a river flows over a cliff, it becomes a waterfall.

Victoria Falls, in Africa

On **limestone** hills, rainwater soaks down through the rock. The water drains into underground rivers, which carve out tunnels and caves.

The Grand Canyon

Millions of years ago, the Colorado River in Arizona began to carve a **valley** out of solid rock. Today, it is called the Grand Canyon. So far, it is 227 miles (365 kilometers) long and up to 18 miles (29 kilometers) wide.

11

River plants

Rivers are good **habitats** for plants because plants need water to grow. Trees that grow alongside rivers have long roots that grip the soil. This helps hold the riverbank together and stop it from being washed away.

Trees grow along a river in a rainforest in Malaysia.

When rivers flow very slowly, some plants grow mostly under the surface of the water. Other plants, such as reeds, have their roots under the water but their leaves grow up into the air above.

Giant water lilies have underwater roots. Their huge leaves float on the surface and can be up to 6.5 feet (2 meters) wide!

Plants are important to the life of a river. Their leaves give off a gas called oxygen, which fish and other river life need to breathe. Plants also provide food for animals and safe places to nest or hide.

Spreading seeds

Many plants rely on rivers to spread their seeds. **Tropical** vines, called lianas, drop their seeds into rivers. The seeds float downstream to the sea and often sprout on distant shores.

Reeds make perfect nests for water birds.

River animals

Rivers are good habitats for animals. They are home to many kinds of fish and amphibians, such as frogs and newts. In warm climates, there are reptiles, such as turtles, crocodiles, and snakes.

Smaller creatures, such as snails, shrimp, beetles, and worms, also live in and around rivers. Many insects, such as dragonflies, live in the water for the first stage of their life. Later, they change into adults and leave the water for a life in the air.

Frog

Ducks

Beetle

Shrimp

Newt

The otter

River otters are active at night, so it is rare to see one during the day. But you might see their droppings, which contain fish bones and scales and smell fishy!

The riverbank is home to many mammals and birds. Mouselike water voles nest in holes in the banks. Water birds nibble plants. Other birds hunt for fish.

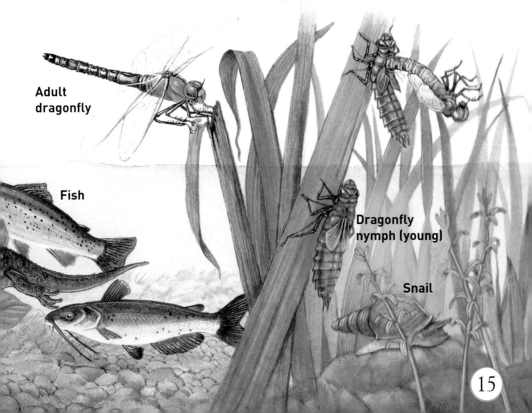

Young dragonfly becomes an adult

Adult dragonfly

Fish

Dragonfly nymph (young)

Snail

Rivers and people

People have always lived next to rivers. Many of the world's oldest and most important cities were built on riverbanks. Cairo is on the Nile River. Rome is on the Tiber River. London is on the Thames River.

Riverside towns and cities have a lot of bridges so people can cross the water. In New York City, a famous bridge called the Brooklyn Bridge links two major parts of the city—Manhattan and Brooklyn—to one another. The bridge runs across the East River.

Every day, thousands of people who live in Brooklyn cross the bridge by car, bus, or on foot to work in Manhattan.

Hundreds of people bathe in the Ganges River in Varanasi, India. This town is an important place for Hindus.

Some rivers have a special meaning for people. The Ganges River in India is **sacred** to **Hindus**, who believe that it washes away their sins. During certain festivals, millions of **pilgrims** travel to the Ganges to bathe in the water.

Using river water

We use river water in many different ways. In our homes, we use it for drinking, washing, flushing the toilet, and watering plants.

Water mills

Water mills have been used on riverbanks for thousands of years. Flowing rivers turned waterwheels. The waterwheels turned heavy stones, which ground grain into flour. This painting shows a water mill from more than 600 years ago.

Factories use huge amounts of river water. They use it to help make things and to cool down machinery when it gets hot. Some farmers take water directly from the river and give it to their animals to drink. They also use it to water their **crops**.

This big machine is watering the crops all around it.

The demand for water is growing and rivers are in danger. When we take too much water from them, fewer plants and animals can live in and around rivers. This affects other animals and people, who rely on them for food.

Rivers and floods

When a river is very full, it overflows and floods the land. This happens when snow melts quickly or heavy rain falls suddenly. The river cannot hold all the water, so it overflows its banks.

Some rivers flood every year. This can be useful for farmers. In India, China, Thailand, and many other countries, rice farmers rely on rivers to flood their rice crops. The water keeps the rice plants cool and controls weeds and pests.

In 2011, heavy rains in Thailand caused dangerous floods. Thousands of people had to leave their homes.

These farmers in Thailand are planting rice in flooded fields.

Unexpected floods are dangerous. They destroy buildings and crops. People and animals may drown. In many parts of the world, people try to prevent flood damage. They build barriers such as **dams** and **dikes** that hold back the water.

Nile River

In ancient Egypt, the Nile River flooded every year. This was very important, as the water and the mud helped crops grow. This was good for Egypt's people.

Dams and water power

A dam is a huge and very strong wall. Dams do more than just hold back river water when it rises. Dams also control the flow of water in other ways.

When a dam is built across a river, it stops the

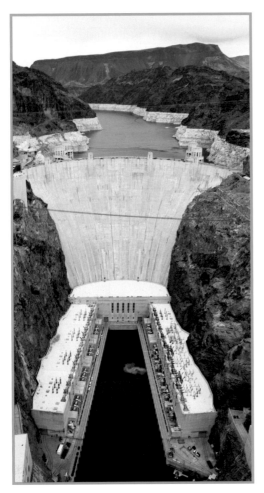

water from flowing downstream. A big lake called a **reservoir** fills in behind the dam. Water is stored in a reservoir so there is always water for local people to use.

The Hoover Dam is on the Colorado River.

The stored water can also be used to make electricity. When water is released through tunnels in a dam, the force of the water turns machines called **turbines**. These drive **generators** that make electricity. A quarter of the world's electricity is made from water power.

Dam

Reservoir

Water in a reservoir

Water from reservoir

The flow of water turns turbines

Problems with dams

Sometimes when a new dam is built, people have to leave their homes to make way for the reservoir. Animals and plants can lose their habitats, too. When the Aswan Dam was built across the Nile River in Egypt, about 200,000 people lost their homes.

River transportation

The longest rivers flow through several countries. Many rivers have been used for a long time to transport people.

Rivers are also useful for transporting **goods**. The Rhine River passes through six countries as it flows toward the North Sea. Huge barges like the one above move up and down the river to factories along its banks. They supply the factories with materials, such as steel and coal, and collect and carry their goods to **port**.

A cruise ship on the Yangtze River in China waits for passengers.

Riverboats come in many shapes and sizes. Small ferries carry people across a river. In cities, tourists board sightseeing boats to get a good view of the sights. Giant cruise ships are like hotels. They carry people along the river for a few days at a time.

River explorers

About 200 years ago, two American explorers, Lewis and Clark, traveled more than 7,770 miles (12,500 kilometers) along rivers to the Pacific coast. It was the first time anyone traveled this far on American rivers.

Enjoying the river

Many rivers are beautiful places where people can relax and have fun. In places where the water flows slowly, people can enjoy swimming or boating. In places where the river flows swiftly, kayaking is a popular river sport.

On warm days, a river's leafy banks are a good place for a stroll or a picnic. You might spot some small animals along the banks or in the water.

Many people enjoy fishing in rivers. Many people catch fish for sport, not food. They catch a fish and then quickly free it from the hook to return it to the water.

Dragon boat races

Many boat races take place on rivers. Dragon-boat racing started in China but has now spread all over the world. Each boat contains up to 20 pairs of rowers and a person who strikes a drum. The rowers have to pull the oars in time to the beating drum.

Putting dirty water in rivers harms plant and animal life.

Taking care of rivers

Rivers are easily **polluted**. Factories pour waste into them that contains harmful chemicals. They also pump warm water into rivers that has been used to cool machines. The warm water is low in oxygen. Both these actions can harm river life.

How to help rivers

- Save water. Here are some tips. Turn off the faucet when you brush your teeth. Collect and use rainwater to water plants instead of tap water.

- Join a group that visits rivers and reports pollution.

- Put litter in trash cans. Litter blows around in the wind and can often end up in rivers.

River clean-ups

Every year there is a national river clean-up day in the United States. Thousands of people all over the country help clean up local rivers. River clean-up day began more than 20 years ago. Since then, almost one million people have participated. More than two million pounds (900 tonnes) of trash have been removed from the water!

Farmers use chemicals called fertilizers to help their crops grow. The fertilizers can also wind up in rivers when it rains. This can cause water plants to grow very fast and upset the balance of the river.

Rivers are very important. They are habitats for wildlife. They provide us with the water we need, and they are beautiful places. Let's keep them clean and healthy!

Glossary

banks the sides of a river

course the path that a river takes

crops plants grown by farmers for food

dams walls built across rivers to hold back the water

dikes low walls, often made of earth, that are built to prevent flooding

erosion the removal of soil and pieces of rock on Earth's surface by water, wind, or ice

estuary the part of the sea that cuts into the land to meet a river's mouth

fresh water water in rivers, lakes, and ice that is not salty like seawater

generators machines that convert movement energy into electrical energy

goods portable items, often those that are for sale

habitats places where animals and plants live

Hindus followers of the Hindu religion

limestone a type of rock

meanders big curves in a river

mouth the place on a river where it enters the sea

pilgrims people on a journey to a sacred place

polluted damaged by waste materials that are unclean and unhealthy

port a town or city with a harbor

recycled used again or made into something new

reservoir a human-made lake that holds water for people to use

riverbed the bottom of a river

sacred special or holy to people of a particular religion

source the place where a river starts

tropical belonging to the tropics—warm, rainy areas of the world

turbines machines that convert movement energy from a liquid into mechanical energy using a series of paddles or buckets

valley an area of low land between hills or mountains

water cycle the movement of water between the Earth's air, the sea, and the land

water vapor water when it has turned into an invisible gas in the air

Index

animals 13, 14–15, 19,
  21, 23, 28, 29

birds 5, 7, 13, 15
boats 24, 25, 26, 27
bridges 16

course 6, 7

D River 5
dams 21, 22–23

electricity 23
erosion 10, 11
estuaries 7
explorers 25

factories 19, 24, 28
farming 19, 20, 25, 29
festivals 17
fish 5, 13, 15, 27
floods 20–21

Ganges River 17
Grand Canyon 11

meanders 7
mills 18

mouth of a river 7
mud 7, 21

Nile River 5, 16, 21

oxygen 13, 28

people 5, 16–17, 18, 19,
  20, 21, 22, 23, 24, 25,
  26, 27, 28, 29
plants 12–13, 18, 20, 29
pollution 28, 29

rain 8, 9, 20, 28
reservoirs 22, 23
riverbanks 5, 10, 12,
  15, 16, 26

sea 7, 8, 13
source 6
sports 4, 26–27

transportation 24–25
underground rivers 11

water cycle 8–9
waterfalls 11

If you have enjoyed reading
this book, look out for more in
the Kingfisher Readers series!

**Collect
and read
them all!**

KINGFISHER READERS: LEVEL 4

The Arctic and Antarctica ☐
Flight ☐
Human Body ☐
Pirates ☐
Rivers ☐
Sharks ☐
Weather ☐

KINGFISHER READERS: LEVEL 5

Ancient Egyptians ☐
Explorers ☐
Hurricanes ☐
Rainforests ☐
Record Breakers—The Fastest ☐
Record Breakers—The Most Dangerous ☐
Space ☐

For a full list of Kingfisher Readers books, plus
guidance for teachers and parents and activities
and fun stuff for kids, go to the Kingfisher Readers
website: **www.kingfisherreaders.com**